Tradit
Crafts of

MEXICO

by Mary Miller

PEARSON

Scott
Foresman

Editorial Offices: Glenview, Illinois • Parsippany, New Jersey • New York, New York
Sales Offices: Needham, Massachusetts • Duluth, Georgia • Glenview, Illinois
Coppell, Texas • Ontario, California • Mesa, Arizona

A Rich, Colorful History

Look around Mexico today, and you'll see colorful cloth, beautiful pottery, and brightly painted murals. These crafts go back thousands of years.

Mexico has a rich history of folk art. A folk artist is someone who makes a traditional craft. These crafts are made by hand in the artist's home. Most artists learn their crafts as children. They learn from family members. In this way, the craft is passed on from generation to generation.

The tradition of Mexican folk art has been passed on for thousands of years.

Ancient Indian Groups

Many Mexican crafts were first made by ancient Indian groups. They are still made the same way today. Some newer craft forms, such as glass blowing, were introduced by the Spanish. But a **glassblower** is rare in Mexico today, so the craft is dying out.

Before explorers from Spain discovered Mexico, powerful Indian groups ruled the land. These ancient peoples were the Maya and the Aztec. They were strong warriors. Their cities had great riches, with large amounts of gold. The Maya and the Aztec also created beautiful craft items.

The ruins of Tenochtitlan, an ancient city, are beneath modern Mexico City.

The Maya

The Mayan civilization was at its peak from about A.D. 250 to A.D. 900. Mayan murals showed lifelike figures taking part in battles and festivals. The artists outlined the figures and then filled them in with color. A similar type of painting was used on Mayan pottery.

The Aztec

The Aztec ruled a mighty empire from 1400 to early 1500. Aztec craftspeople used feathers to make beautiful clothes and headdresses. Other important Aztec crafts were weaving, metalworking, pottery, and woodcarving.

Mayan artists decorated walls and buildings with brightly colored murals.

Today, traditional Mexican crafts are made all over Mexico. You can find pottery in Mixteca, woven baskets in Veracruz, and masks in Oaxaca. You can find beautiful embroidered cloth in Acapulco. Every region has its own specialty.

Modern Mexican Crafts

In the 20th century, many poor people left the countryside to find **factory** jobs in the city. Some traveled on foot, and others came on **burros**.

But not all things made in Mexico today come from factories. In the villages, Mexican folk artists still make crafts. They work in the same way as the ancient peoples of Mexico.

Folk artists take their crafts to the village market to sell to tourists.

Mexican Pottery

Pottery is one of the oldest crafts in Mexico. Most Mexican pottery is made by hand. The clay pieces are shaped and then dried. The dried pieces are then painted with geometric patterns.

In the countryside, ancient ways of making pottery are still used today. For example, Mixteca Indian women still dig clay from the earth. They use this clay to make bowls, cups, and dishes. Sometimes they make vases, statues, or flutes to **puff** into and play a simple **tune**. After the clay pieces dry out in the air, they are fired in an open pit. Until they are fired, they must be handled carefully so they do not **burst**.

Traditional Mexican potters shape clay by hand.

After the pottery is fired, the bright colors are painted on by hand.

When the Spanish arrived, the native Indian groups learned new ways to make pottery.

One type of pottery is made only in Puebla, Mexico. This glazed, or shiny, pottery has been made the same way for nearly 500 years. Originally, blue was used on only the finest pieces because the color was very expensive. Other colors, such as green and yellow were introduced in the 1700s.

This pottery is prized for its beautiful shade of blue.

Oaxacan Black Pottery

Oaxacan potters use black clay to make their pottery. Special techniques are used to polish these pieces. The fine patterns on each piece are cut out by hand.

The region of Oaxaca is known for its black pottery.

Weaving

Indians were weaving in the valleys of Oaxaca as long ago as 500 B.C. After they were taken over by the Aztec, their woven clothes became valuable.

Today, Oaxacan weavers still create beautiful wool rugs. Each rug is woven by hand on a loom. Many weavers use natural dyes. The colors come from animals, plants, and minerals. These dyes produce beautiful colors that do not fade or rub off.

An artist can work for 300 hours to create one rug.

Basket Weaving

Weaving beautiful and useful things from reeds and palm leaves is one of Mexico's oldest crafts. Weavers use Mexican bamboo and palm leaves to make baskets, hats, and mats.

The weavers use natural dyes to color the reeds and leaves in deep shades of blue, red, and purple. The dyed reeds are then woven by hand into beautiful patterns. In some Veracruz towns, women can weave as many as twenty baskets a day.

Weaving has changed very little over thousands of years.

13

Masks

People in Mexico have been making masks for thousands of years. The first known mask was made about 12,000 B.C. The mask looked like a coyote's head. Many masks were made of gold and precious stones, such as turquoise and coral.

The Spanish introduced the custom of wearing masks at dances. Today, masks are worn in Mexico during festivals and celebrations. Some masks look like animals. Some masks are carved from wood and painted in bright colors. Other masks are made from colorful beads. Often, masks are decorated with colorful feathers for hair.

A mask from Teotihuacan

Mexicans still perform a dance called the *Tezcatlipoca*, or "smoking mirror." This dance is named for Tezcatlipoca, an invisible god who is shown as a black mirror. Tezcatlipoca's special animal was the jaguar. Dancers wear jaguar masks with mirrors set in the eyeholes.

Mexican people wear masks like this at traditional dances.

Wood Carving

During their rule, the Maya and Aztec peoples carved wood to make useful objects and decorations. Today, craftspeople carve wooden figures called *alebrijes*. These are Mexico's newest craft form. They were first made in small towns in Oaxaca fifty years ago. Often, these carvings show animals, fantastical creatures, or monsters. They are carved one at a time by hand, so no two carvings are ever the same.

Once a carving is done, the figure is painted in bright colors.

Needlework

Needlework is highly prized in Mexican culture. Many people wear shirts embroidered with bright colors and patterns. Most embroidery work is done by women. Girls learn needlework at a young age from their mothers and grandmothers. There are many beautiful embroidery designs.

People in Mexico wear their embroidery with pride.

The Art of the Day of the Dead

Do you think skeletons are scary? Most Mexicans would **reply** that they are not. On November 2, people in Mexico celebrate *Dia de los Muertos*, or "Day of the Dead." Many Mexicans believe that death is not final. Rather, it is part of the cycle of life.

As with many events in Mexico, Dia de los Muertos has produced a tradition of craft forms. Artists make small, bright skeletons to sell. Many skeletons are made from papier-mâché. These happy skeletons are shown doing the activities people enjoy every day.

Flowers are placed on graves as part of the Dia de los Muertos celebration.

A traditional
papier-mâché
skeleton

19

Glossary

burros *n.* small donkeys

burst *v.* to break open suddenly

factory *n.* a building where things are made or built

glassblower *n.* a person who blows air into a heated lump of glass to make shapes

puff *v.* to blow in short breaths

reply *v.* to respond to an activity or answer a question

tune *n.* a piece of music; a melody